CHILLED LOVE

CRIME GENRE POEM

SELVARAJ ARUNACHALAM

Contents

Preface

Selvaraj Arunachalam is a veteran crime journalist. He has been covering crime and police since 1994. He works as an assistant editor-crime in The Times of India. He had also worked in Daily Thanthi, The New Indian Express, and Deccan Chronicle Holdings Limited. He unearthed breaking stories including Divya Mataji's arrest in Tiruchi, mobile thieves being forced to perform unnatural sexual act inside T Nagar police station in police custody and many more...

Prologue

Many poems portray love, dejected love, nature, mother's love, sentiments, and so on.

Is it possible to bring suspense and crime thriller resonating with love through poetry?

Crime writing and poetry are like a sword and a sickle or a 9mm pistol and a grenade.

All these years, he tracked and followed criminals and police personnel.

The idea of creating this crime genre poem is to narrate a short film through the poem that has an

etymological and thematic connection.

Contents

1. MY FIRST ALIEN TRIP

Enter Caption

I notice a naughty girl
At the loop of immigration check

Her eyes shimmer in excitement
Her hand holds firmly
The handle popped out of a suitcase
She turns and spills a smile at her pals
I see her looking at a chubby diaper-girl
The playful girl's eyes widen
Twitches her lips to bite the kid's cheek
She pinches air as if nipping the child
She makes gentle noise with her tongue
'Tock-Tuck'…
Everyone in queue turns
She ignores all eyes
Looks at fatty child
She smiles at her
And stretches her hands upwards in the air
Makes a 'Hurray' sign
As people look strange and weird
She purses her lips
And blushes
Even after I take a 'U' in the loop
Her smiling eyes gleam through my heart
I don't want to forget the pair of eyes
I close my lids to recap again and again
'Excuse me' – the man holds his suitcase on the left hand
Opens his right arm gently
I shake my head
Acknowledging with a smiling apology

Move front to the immigration officer
I show my passport
Officer asks tailor-made queries
I give expected replies
Show appointment at Royal Brompton hospital in SL
As the officer stamps a green seal
Pluck the passport
My eyes scan for the girl
See her cat-walking upright
Rush to corridors; Eyes continue to search
I hear the 'tock-tuck' echoes
From a duty-free dress shop
Walk-in and see her eyes glitters
As a mermaid dress flows on her from neck to toe
Announcement flows through the speakers
I see 'Boarding Now'
For British Airways flight
Walkthrough cubicle to enter the tube
Search for 'M' row – aisle seat
Leave my hand luggage inside the header
I walk into the washroom and return
See the 'spicy-girl' next to my seat
My heart pounds rapidly
She sits next to me
To hide my excitement; I turn
My face quickly to the other side
And breathe-in chunk of air

Till my lungs turn cold
Moist my lips
And walk back to my seat
I spill smile at her
She looks and turns towards the window
'No response' – shame on me
She looks at tiny airport buildings
And smiles extra-large
I help her to buckle-up
She smiles and focuses back
She jumps like a child travelling on a roller coaster,
As flight rolls towards the runway
She stays put outside
Her excitement is missing now
As the bird climbs on air
She screams in a nightmare
I pat at her hand mildly
She grasps my hand tightly
Till the birds fly high above clouds
I feel like floating in space
She now discloses a pure smile
Acknowledging me
My heart vein blasts inside
Notwithstanding excessive blood circulation
Blood oozes out of my nose
Crew members call for doctors travelling
She screams

An elderly man examines

It's 'Cardiac arrest'

But it's 'Cardiac explosion'

She screams again…

It's my first ever alien trip…

****

2. FROZEN LOVE

Enter Caption

My body moves in rhythm

My eyes fix on the mirror

Like an owl

It reflects me

White hair sprouts through my wrinkled cheek

I feel myself a 62-yr-old boy

I flex my forearm

Skeleton pushes up my dry skin

I stand on the pathway

Wind gushes through the half-opened train door

I stare at the mirror and try to sneak-in

Almost two decades ago…

I lean my head on her shoulder

Her right-hand cuddles up to my left arm, While

Her left-hand busy strokes through my hair

I look at the mirror

I couldn't see her face

As spouting air creates pencil art on her

A man wearing a black coat

Asks me to go to a coupe

I return

Bury my body inside a woollen bed sheet

Close my eyes in search of fairy tales; But

The scenery runs in front of my closed eyes

Like a negative film

My eyeballs roll left and right

Till white abdicates the whole screen

I wake up from a dream; As

Someone knocks at the coupe door

Come out to see a skinny elderly porter

Any help sir? – his voice chokes

I nod my head

He takes a bag on his shoulder

Walks out with a briefcase

I follow him As I walkthrough

A recorded female voice says

Welcome to 'Madurai Junction'

He asks, "Where are you going, sir?"

I say instantly – 'Hotel Blue Mountain'

He stares at me, asks, "It's not that good."

Glances at me again

The man drops me at the hotel lobby

I show my card to the receptionist

He takes note of formalities

He presses the caller button

Puny boy arrives skating barefoot

He shows me to the second floor

Room number '203'

Lock the room; Open the window

It shrieks due to ageing

Vehicle noise on road hushes it

Return to bed

I roll on the hard mattress

The bed has been shifted diagonally

Recollecting the memories
Added one more wardrobe and chair
Burnt cigarette and stinking smell choke my lungs
I go near the six-foot huge mirror
I turn back
She sleeps in a bed-sheet cocoon
Her bare legs pop out of it
I sit next to her and lean
She rolls gently
To engulf my body into her
As I know her weak points
I prod on them
She giggles and pushes me away
I retaliate to avoid falling
She loses her hold and
Falls hit on a metal body
It's a plate with fruits and a glass of water
I look at the ceiling and realise
Get up 'My Love'
She remains silent
Crawl to peep off the bed
See her in the pool of blood
Her eyes wide open
Staring at the mirror
See deep injury on the throat, warmblood oozes out
Inflicted by the knife kept on the bananas
I try to stand on my legs

As I fell; As the floor underneath was moving,
I swoon
Wake up to buzzer noise
Whirrrrr….
Tears roll out my eyes
'My Love' is dead
Walk to the door
Peep through the eyehole
See a room serviceman with a jug
I scream, "I will call back."
Whirr… stops
A man walks, his steps fade as he climbs down the staircase
I sweat profusely through all my skin pores
My heart beats fast
I give instruction to my mind to react
Decide and step out
I return with a huge suitcase
And a cap
To cover my face
Both my palms turn wet suddenly
I take the knife and slide
It inside a small hole behind the mirror
Apply floor cleaner and keep everything as it is
I check out the room with 'my love'
Bundled inside the suitcase
Board the train from Madurai to Chennai
Braved myself recollecting crime thrillers

Push 'my love' into river Cauvery, which was brimming

Thanks to Karnataka CM SR Bommai

She drowns in River Cauvery

The next day, it was on the headlines

"WOMAN FOUND DEAD INSIDE SUITCASE"

The news reads someone noticed it at Kallanai Dam

Newsmakers later move on to the 'Sivakasi' Jayalakshmi case

Due to ageing, the events fade away from my mind

Not her memories…

It was the same mirror

I touch and feel the mirror

I thrust my finger behind the mirror

To check out for the hole

Something hit at my fingers

Some sensation excerpts shock

Instantly to the back of my head

I return to bed

Lean on it

Clock shrieks

I walk towards the mirror again

Struggle to take the knife out

It was rusted near the handle

I touch 'my love's' blood clotted and turned hard

Like my mind 20-years ago

I keep the sharp side of knife on my throat

And look at the mirror

Room bell rings – this time a bird chirp

I turn my head towards the door

A 'thud' noise hears near my ears

I turn towards the mirror

Before I react, the huge wardrobe falls on me

I bury under huge 100-kgs of wooden planks

Minutes later,

The room boy and hotel staffs break open door

Five people remove the wardrobe

I was under it

The sharp edge of the knife slices my throat

Warm blood mixes up with 'MY FROZEN LOVE'

I was blacked-out

As people whispers into my ears…

Rush him to hospital, he is still alive…

I know I am dying…

As blood gushes out of wound…

****

3. ETERNAL JOURNEY

Enter Caption

It's quarter past 6
Sky cracks in the east
Leaks blood; That spill
On sponges, flies up and up
Turns into clouds
It's my first assignment
I open the kit
Birds fly high in the sky
I see the flocks through a viewfinder
'Click', 'Click'…
Rolls digitally, As camera shutter
Swallows hastily in one-tenth of a flicker
"Hello," – familiar voice chokes, my breathe
Voice follows by 'Victoria Secret' fragrance
It's she…
I wave my hand, without turning back
"Hi,"
She lifts her eyebrows forming
Turtled 'V'
It sutures my heart, seeing
Platinum ring pierces above her right eyebrow
She laughs wide
Exposes her gingivae
"I want to tell you something,"
And turn back; To open-up my mind's nostril
See her climbing into a TNSTC bus
I follow her

Jasmine flower smell flows deep into my lungs
Makes tipsy without taking fermented grape juice
Music director Deva's folk song
Deafens unwanted speeches in bus
A man gives a seat for me
'Praise the Lord'
She wears brown-coloured trouser-skirt
And a white t-shirt with pony-tailed hair
As she shakes her head,
Hair follows her like my mind
The bus starts its journey
From Chennai-Koyambedu to Kancheepuram
She narrates her project
She excited to meet refugees in the camp
Her eyes glitter in excitement
As it comes true after following hectic procedures
I wait for a moment, which never comes
Bus shakes again as if suffered 'cardiac arrest'
The driver pulls over to left
All passengers wait on the roadside
And we too…
Witnessing vehicles passing through
Like an unprofessional violinist
Pulling strings to high and short notes
As for trucks cross, the earth under our feet shakes
Expressing a mild tremor
I see a tractor approaches us

Some people board the trailer

We decide to travel with them

I get a place next to groom; And

She sits next to the bride

I spill a friendly smile on 20 pairs of eyes

Some girls giggle at me; Whisper

I open my kit

She purses her lips

Her gestures expose me

As a smart chatterbox

I capture the groom with a flowery cap

We sit on a bed sheet; But

Cow dung and grass straw aroma/odour still remains

Capture bride and my girl in unique poses

She notices it,

Chides by biting her tongue gently

"When will we reach camp?" she asks in sign language

I turn my left wrist

Watch displays 7.20 A.M.

I reply to her, "Before 8.00 A.M"

I appreciate the tractor driver for manoeuvring

The traffic signboard says, "Sunguvarchathiram – 1 Km ahead"

Huge 'THUD' noise at the front

Seconds later, my camera flies in the air,

With auto-recording mode turns on

A huge tanker truck collided head-on with a tractor

Tanker overhead-valve breaks; liquid pops out
Sweet-smelled colourless liquid spills on us
Within nanoseconds, the place turns an inferno
Fire eats 'Benzene' sticker and truck
I twist my head to see 'my girl'
Everywhere dense black smoke
I hear a feeble voice, 'help', 'help'…
It's her voice
Again a 'THUD' noise
This time, the tanker explodes
Scattering people all over
As benzene chemical sneaks into my eyes
I can't see around
Move towards her thinning voice
I scream in pain
People everywhere cry and howl
I search for her
I crawl and extend my hands frantically
Touching still-people lying down
Identifies her, as ring clings on her forehead
I…'I want to say something'…
Ambulance siren screams closely
Regain blurred vision at one of my eyes
Masked paramedics lift me on a stretcher
"Rescue her," I scream in delicate voice to them…
Turn back in search of her
Her eyes wide open and stare at me

Her torso is charred
As I enter the ambulance
My limbs turn numb, due to air-conditioner
Below my waist, charred limbs, and breaks
Hungry death slowly eats my vital parts
And my heart, finally
My eternal journey begins with her…

****

4. iCLOUD...

Enter Caption

Alarm shrieks in my mobile
Sound waves hit the ear drum mildly
Echoes as if trapped in a black hole
Head spins twice
My left arm extends
Searching for phone
Presses its ears to snooze
I blink my eyes
Everything looks blurred
Lift head up
Rotating fan makes shadow art
My right arm impulsively moves
Fingers run on the forehead
Eyes, nose, Fingers…stretch out
Halts for a second
The mind takes control.
Instruct hands
Comb table for my glasses
Switch on laptop
While it boots up.
Yawn like roaring
Blacked out for a few seconds
Digital clock blinks.
It's 5 a.m.
Enter her name.
'Matilda' at the search menu
Facebook spits out a list

No result found

She is nowhere in 'iCloud'

I close my eyes again

Morning Prayer echoes in the air

My bodyweight lies on one leg

Right arm clings on metallic railing

The bus travels from Madurai to Trichy

Men, women; 'Unity in diversity

Many expect for a motel to come

See her for the first time

She leans between seat and railing

Notice 'villain' behind her

He touches, moves away from her in inches

Repeats it again; Again —

He proves Newton's third law

I step in to help her

Lock his body with one leg

She turns back

Her eyes flicker

I visualise myself as a 'hero'

Hold my balance

Her humble eyes thank me

I find a seat for her

Coconuts bundle in a gunny bag

I ask her name; 'Matilda'

Her name echoes.

Doorbell rings

'Sorry for the break'
Walk, see paperboy
Return to bed, leaving the paper on a table
Close my eyes
Emptying lung
See her at college
Meet at Rockfort; Rock restaurant,
Chat, walk-in pair around temple tank
She speaks self, Orphan
Lives with 'villain' uncle
Grows up; Wants to marry
She gleams through my eyes
Asks me
"Will you marry me?"
I nod my head up-down in rhythm
She cheers up
The semester ends; goes back home
My mobile rings
It's she; 'Can we marry now?'
I pause to answer
She hangs on phone
Disappears into thin air
Snooze ends
Phone alarm rings again
I walk to washroom
I touch my bald head
Silver hair encroaches all over

Skin turns loose

With lot of dead tissues

Look up to see mirror

I am 71…

My search never ends for her

She is alive somewhere in 'iCloud'

A line of light across heavens

"Come on in my flying machine" …

Two days later…

Neighbours complain of foul smell

Cops arrive, retrieve corpse

Laptop screen unlocks…

Mouse handle hit search button

For 'Matilda'…

****

5. GRAVITY...

Enter Caption

My path makes footprints on dusty road
Breeze breaches into my heart
Feel aroma behind me
It's her favourite
Her jingle voice echoes
"I won't make friends
I don't trust anyone"
Why are you behind me?
Mind says, Head rolls 180 degrees
No one's there
"Good morning, sir"
A boy screams through my ears
I enter the village-school
One huge hall, all students stand up
Says in chorus, "Good Morning"
As I drop my 65 kgs into wooden chair
I smell for my beloved scent
Nothing comes, Except oiled head smell
And lunch sambar
I return home before dusk
Feel her following me again
Pull out mobile
Ring her number
It says not reachable
Call her friend, mobile rings
No answer
Rush to home

Sweat leaks from my palms

Rub it too trouser

Sweat again that glitters in evening sun

This is not the first time

Fall into melancholy

Rush to meet parents in city

Inform my friend

Take a Valium tablet to rest my nerves

Wake up as something chokes my neck

Walk to the table

Drink some water

As it spills, searches for napkin towel

See a diary on table

Open it, see a folded newspaper

My heart beats strange

Blood booms from toe to head

News report about an accident

With her smiling picture

And mangled bike

Close the diary

Hear unusual echoes behind my ears

Balls roll

Criss-cross into my stomach

Feel as if at high altitude

Suffocate and hard to breathe

Take two more pills

To put my soul and body to sleep

Next day.

Friend follows me secretly

To track her

As I step out on to road

Feel like her following me once more

Closely, very closely…

I scream in freaky voice

Friend follows me, panics

Chillness spread fast across my stomach

Collapse down, faint

Beep…beep…voice

And hospital smell flows into my lungs

My friends speak mildly behind the screen

Hears clearly

He explains

Doctor, "It's his shadow"

"He fears of his shadow, thinking of her"

"He says it's her, following him"

But One good thing

He forgets accident

Gory death of her witnessing him…

My head spins fast

As if sitting at the front row in ferries wheel

Roll and fall from bed

A pair of scissors punctures my heart

Fresh blood runs

Towards gravity…

SELVARAJ ARUNACHALAM

****

6. NO MOON DAY…

Enter Caption

I open my eyes
Sun rays suck my energy
Lower my face, closing lids
Her face appears before me
I lift my hand
The shadow disappears
It's like a no moon day
Tears profusely roll down my cheeks
I hide my tears under dark sunglass
Walk towards the train
Follow army man's footpath
Crushing of sand by hard boots
Her memories hit my mind again
My upper eyelids shutter
Like a panicked butterfly stuck in a web
Eyes itch as if
Minute-stone granules fall into it
Open my left hand to hold something
Get hold of a railing at a bogey
Hold it for a minute
Hand shivers mildly
Hold my breath; Release it slowly
Till my lungs suffocate
Mind the steps to get in the bogey
Wrongly steps on to air
Fall forward
Bangs on train's metal body

Falls; Feels like a dark valley in front of me
A soft tender hand holds me
'Can't you be little careful' –
Gentle voice flows through the air
Fiddles through my ears
I said, 'Sorry' and 'Thank You'
Mostly used words; I hate them
I touch her thumb finger softly
Her nail looks flat on top, with Slopes on both sides
I run my index finger on her nail
A ball of air chokes my throat
I walk in holding my boarding ticket
She sees it
Shows way towards my seat
'Yeah', she exclaims
Realise later, it's next to her
She chatters non-stop
I want to fiddle through her nail softly
I stand up; hit my leg and am about to fall
She extends her arms towards me
Her moisturiser smells close
Shows her cleanliness, Caring of health
My whole body vibrates mildly
Stomach draws back in jolt
I imagine her face as square
With narrowed down
Broad smile exposing her gums

She laughs in instalments
I bend my face little
To hear her voice clearly
She might be less than five-foot
May be in early 30s'
Her wrists and forearms are strong
Showing her agile
Faces hard and tough times
I said, "Sorry, again".
It's okay; it's not mine
Confirms as error-less girl
She's a butterfly
Opening her wings to fly far away
The train noise gushes through the window
Hampers her gentle voice
I sleep on the bed as her voice still echoes
Wake up as a tough hand touches my cheeks
I search for her
Pin drop silence in the coach
The man shakes my hand again
He lifts my baggage
Guides me to out of the train
He said, "Train reaches long back."
'Did you take any drug, last night?'
I shook my head negatively
Everyone leaves the station except you
I search you in all bogeys

His voice diminishes

Somewhere in long, I hear her voice

Fading away further and further

He opens his bag

Unwraps a cover

It's a smart blind stick…

He unlocks, gives it to me

I put on dark sunglass again…

****

7. LAST RIDE TOGETHER

Enter Caption

I flip over my wrist
Look at my watch

Two minutes past 6
Flies and birds rush back home
As gloom abdicates the earth into darkness
Couple of flies collide head-on helmet visor
Die on the spot
I am a slayer
Close my eyelids for quarter in a second
Kneel before a priest
Seek pardon for my negligent sin
His voice echoed behind the net
'I absolve your sins'
Lift my head from the mesh
There's no one inside the wooden enclosure
I miss a tanker narrowly
Whizzzz…
Passes me and horn fades away
Giant's rapid movement creates temporary vacuum
Bike judders as if caught in air-pocket
See my girl stands at a bus stop
Her eyes scan the passers-by quickly
Searches for me; I assume
Her nose tip glitters in the descending sun light
It blacks out my vision for a second
Her lips twitch and eyelids flutter
I come close to her
She showers her ray of light on me quickly
Spills a small smile

Her lips widen half-a-centimetre
Sits on the pillion
My grip on handlebars tightened
Stretch out my arms as if going to lift weight
Sucks air to bloat my lungs
Her perfume fills my lung
It thrills sniffing raw drug
Bike floats in air
She holds and extends her arms around my waist
Her screams resonate from a deep well
She shakes my shoulders tightly
I park my bike and then
Open my eyes widely
We are on the top of a flyover
Sun descends further on the west
She whispers
Let's 'break up'
She repeats in mild note
Let's 'break up'
She asks me to get down from bike
My heart pauses a second to pump blood
Arteries and nerves dry up lack of body fluid
She gently lifts her shoulders
'I like you more than this world' – she whispers again
Let's go for a long ride
She sits on the rider seat
I sit carefully on pillion

Hold her shoulders softly

Offer to wear headgear; she rejects

Drives fast, as her hair strands strangle my neck

My soul wants to leave

To the eternal world

Far away and away

A fly rush back home

Falls into one of her eyes

She lifts both her hand

Screams in agony

I push my body forward

Hold the accelerator to reduce the speed

I search for the brakes

I was late

Bike hits wall on flyover

Flies into barren lake

Full of empty liquor bottles strewn everywhere

The last ride together

For me; It's

A happy ride together…

****

8. SIGAPPI...

Enter Caption

I still remember her

She stands near a bike showroom

I see her

She looks a little dusty

Her nose glitters in moonlight

I ask her name

She speaks

Whirr..whirr…

Her voice fades away in moving air

Once I reach the house

I turn around

I call her – Sigappi

She keeps silent, heads down

I wake up to *subrabatham* echoes from a temple

It's nearing six

I search for Sigappi

I see her at the portico

Sigappi looks bright

Wears red dupatta

There is no one around

I place my hand around her hip

I feel her cold abdomen

She doesn't deny

I smile and blush

The day limps slowly for me

I run out of the office

I see her standing at the bike parking

I rush to her
Guard stops me
He gives a letter
I hold it
Through the open side
A photo slide down
A woman poses as 'Madonna' smiles 'at me'
'At those' who look at the photo
I turn towards 'Sigappi'
She turns her head on the opposite side
Her eyes welled
Tears roll and fall on crease spilt on road, turns black
I put my leg around her
To convince
I utter the magical words 'I Love You'
No reply, no nod – from her
I return home
She doesn't even spell a word
After reaching home
I want to take revenge on her
I don't even see her back
I go to my room
I keep the photo cover under the table mat
Sigappi doesn't turn up
I wash my body and return
No trace of her in the room
Victoria's secret smell is missing

Mobile phone rings

Amma's photo pops up

Swipe the green circle upwards

My mother's voice flows through

"Ma, will you listen to me, please"

No, I've decided her as my in-law

I feel Victoria's secret smell

I swiftly turn in a reflex action

Door remains open

Curtains waves in the breeze

No one is inside the room

"Mom screams on the other side"

"Yes, Ma…why do u scream?"

Okay, da… I am happy now, I arrange everything, next week's marriage…

"But, ma, I said Okay for" …Beep, beep, beep…

Phone disconnected on the other side

I look strangely on the phone

Climb down

The door was opened

Sigappi still stands there near the portico

Hey, Sigappi, sorry dear…

I was careful to avoid her eyes

Our love doesn't even stay for a day

A car honks at the entrance

CCTV camera shows a woman in the car

Guard lets the car into the house

She gets down
She looks the same in the photo
She introduces me
"I am Deepu" …
"Hi, I am Shiv" …
"Nice to see you," …
My voice chokes in middle
I speak in a husky voice…
As Sigappi is there…
Turn back and stop for a while
She is not there now
My eyes frisk all over and search for her
Turn around,
As Deepu touches my shoulder
She speaks
"I stay in women's hostel"
"I come here with a request"
"Will you take me to my friend's house"
She opens her car
And returns with a gift
"Is it for me" … speak myself
"No," she replies
How does she read my mind's voice?
"You will have something more" …
Deepu winks and smiles like Priya Varrier
She says, "It's for my friend"
On her birthday…

I get an excuse for two minutes
To dress up
Returns with a cowboy dress
I put the hat on to her
And I wear headgear
My heart beats fast
As Deepu rolls her hands around me
Raise the throttle to cross 100 km/hr
Ignore red indication – cross barriers
A bike runs faster than a horse
I turn my wrist to see the time
It shows 11.40 PM
My heart gallops in danger
As the brake cable snaps
I sweat profusely
A Taurus lorry from behind hit the bike
The bike hits hard on median
I flow in the air
Cowboy hat flows ahead
Turn around and search for her
Deepu falls on-road and she runs towards me
I am happy, she is safe
I crash-landed on my right hand
I feel some bones break inside
I spill a smile at Deepu
She smiles, and her smile disappears instantly
She stares at me in danger

I realise landed on the opposite side of the road
A container hit
BANG…
Crushed my stomach, coughs up blood
Tastes my own blood
It's my last breath
I believe I deserve it for cheating 'Sigappi'
Deepu faints
Cops arrive at the accident spot
Sketches using chalk on the road
A policeman scribbles
Lorry number KA 05 AS 5235
Container heads from south to north
Bike number TN 45 F 0186
Model Hero Honda CD-100
"Red colour and 1996 make the engine,"
A policeman examines and says
Brake cable snaps and causes accident
The policeman examines the scene
He looks strange
The engine is not running
But still, headlight blinks
"Sir", he calls another policeman
The engine is shut sir, but still…
Now rush to the hospital
Check for the bike key
The policeman searches for the key

An onlooker brings a key
Sir, please check if it is this bike's key
Drops the key in a plastic cover
The key chain has 'SIGAPPI' embossed letters
"BLAST" …
The bike bursts and flies high
Falls on the opposite side of the road
Where Shiv's body was lying some time ago
The headlamp blinks for the last time…

****

9. AN ODE TO MOM

This Is an Ode to All Moms in This World!

I feel the earth under my feet

Whisking away

I feel like standing on edge of the land

A blue whale

And buries into huge water around

Traveling in a bus without base

I leave a seat next to me vacant

It's for my mom

She is no more; But she is alive

I look at the fast-moving greenery

Looks like a water colour painting

My eyes have opened wider

Only black image falls on my retina

Try to divert my anguish

Looking into the picturesque

My eye lids have turned huge iron sheet

No relation or regrets – Still

My eyes turn pool of tears

I swim in the tears for hours

Finally, I fall off rolling on

Steep-slope Cheek

She is no more; But she is alive…

****

10. NEVER ENDING DAWN

It's going to be never-ending dawn to celebrate your birthday!!Happy Birthday to My Dear

OH, BUTTERFLY!
Take me over the clouds
To celebrate your Birthday first
As soon as Sun arises on the horizon
And I wanna celebrate the feast whole day
Travelling ahead of the dawn
That wakes every life on earth
Oh, Butterfly!
Take me to the sky
To pour blossoms on earth
To form new bloom islands
To mark your Birthday
OH, BUTTERFLY!
Take me above earth's gravity
To celebrate your Birthday
Across all latitudes and longitudes of the globe
OH, BUTTERFLY!
Take me under the earth
I wanna sleep permanently
To keep the earth below your footpaths
As warm forever!
OH, BUTTERFLY!
Leave me your colour on my hand
I wanna fly like you and vanish in thin air
To mix up into you breathe
To fill in you, forever!

OH, BUTTERFLY!

Open your wings

You've never opened it so wide

Creating shadow roofs for homeless

Leads live as thou birds clipped and caged

OH, BUTTERFLY!

Fly too high altitude

Above gravity as thou your attitude

To float in space

To explore aliens in the cosmos

OH, UNCHAINED BUTTERFLY!

You are free now and always

Don't bewilder humans

And always be cautious about humans

Many yet to acquire humanely

Don't fall prey to loneliness

OH, BUTTERFLY!

Open your windows

Breathe fresh breeze

Try flying before stepping out into wild

Pollens and honey in flowers attract you

To trap and clip your wings

Take your old house 'Cocoon'

To play hide and seek

Enjoy the world that's so high!

The world so high!

****

11. BROKEN FEATHERS

Enter Caption

Mild flapping noise
Wakes me from a nap
My eyelids struggle to open
See a butterfly flying
Away and far away
Feel the insect on my index finger
It shed colour on me
I smile at a butterfly that flies far
I close my eyes again
My eyeballs pan on both ends.
Jump like a tide
I refine my ears
To trace waning flap sound
The flapping sound comes closer
It wakes me up again
An arm extends
Grabs me off an auto
My head lifts 45 degrees
I see my face amidst the clean sky
It's my offspring
I spill a friendly smile
Exposing my canine teeth
He grabs my hand
I look at my hand
Wrinkles form modern art
All over my body
Spinal cord turns as a bow

I struggle to walk

Two more pair of hands help me

Bail out from iron auto doors

Strange hand releases me

Known pair of hands

Warmly wraps my hand

Three fingers pat me gently

I lift my head up

As I again hear the flap sound

My heart beats happily

She – butterfly – is with me

The fly circles me merrily

Hops on and off flowers in shrubs

Sun gleams through my eyes

I put down my head.

Close my eyes

Memories run down past 30 years

I walk across grass lawn

I hold a tender hand

It's my progeny

As he lands on a pit

I feel him sinking like

A float connects to fishing rod

Slings his hand up

Holding his one hand

He pounces on my shoulder

Hear flap sound close to my heart

Memory disappears

I return to the day as if.

Heavy punch hit my heart –

Hear the insect fretting hard

See a noose traps butterfly

My mind falls gloomy

Butterfly turns sombre

I lift my head

I read 'Mercy Home' board

It welcomes me

See anxious people behind bars

I am now one among them

Flap sound vanishes

My car roars silently behind me

Silence behind me!

****

12. LAST BENCH GIRL

Enter Caption

Puny girl fiddles her plait
She sinks into reveries
As protégé start jotting on their class note
She closes it
Cacophony leaks through the ledge
Boisterous pitter-patter on ground
Close to her heart
Her mind falls pensive
Teacher wakes her up with a question
She blanches
Her mind shakes with glee
She gazes through teacher's eyes
As bell rings in her dream
She struts out to humongous ground
She sees pupil slurp
And plonk the bottles
Her eyes hastily search for clan
Runs frantically streaking
Diagonally ploughs through ground
Sees vicious fray with din
Makes a lunge stealthily
Wakes up nigh to growl again
She blinks closing her eyes for a second
She is in front of the teacher
Poses charlatan and scowls
Retreats to avoid a whack from rotund tutor
Tickles as she glares and frowns

Runs away and never turns up
Impassive she is now Stateswoman…

****

13. SIGN LANGUAGE

Enter Caption

Chirping birds give a strange look at me
I am waiting.
Waiting on a bench in the park
It's early even before dawn
Sun yet to spread its wings on earth
The priest prepares for the Morning Prayer
The woman walks with some chalk to draw kolam
At every doorstep on the street
Early before guard with a handle-bar moustache
He walks behind bushes
And returns with his gray uniform
I look at my watch
Thin needle kisses
Both big and small needles every 60 seconds
I watch it proudly as if I've invented it
The morning breeze flows gently
Indicating her arrival
Pot-bellied people walk frantically with headgears plugged
I look at her
She nods her head
As she notices my blushing
She looks bright as ever
She ignores it as a bad joke
After staring at her for long
Even after Sun moves to wake up people
On the other side of the earth
She turns back

As she hears her friends behind the bushes

They give a gentle look to return home

I'm talking to her expressionless.

Motionless through my eyes

Suddenly air traps in my throat

Rolls up and down

Blocking my vocal cord

I use saliva to push it back into my stomach

My tongue dries up

I am choked

Mildly opened my mouth to live for her

As words queue up below air bubble

Tears emerge from my eyes

It forms like depression in the Bay of Bengal

She looks at me

I suck the tears into my eyes

I cover my face

As if wiping off sweat

Wipe off the tear droplets

See her missing in front of me

She flies back with her friends

While fasting like me

Without tasting honey from flowers

She flies away and far away from me

She never turns back…

****

14. EERIE FEVER...

Enter Caption

A woman vendor screams

Her gravelly voice

Shrieks: Dissolve in space

Depreciates further, flows into my ears

I wake up to her cries

Antique clock door screeches and opens

Metallic bird peeps out

Mimic to stored chirp voice

I open my eyes at slow pace
I feel like sand granules
Rolling hard under the eyelids
I count the chirps carefully
It ends after five times twice
I stretch my body underneath bed
Burning heat waves warmth trapped air
Catnap drags my soul to fairy garden
I see birds talking instead of chirping
Feel like floating
Amidst live animated characters
My eyes scan around quickly
If I were inside 'Disney' studio
A butterfly approaches me
She bows her head little
With her eyes close and open
Like a noiseless camera shutter
I recap her reactions into slow motion
I get ample time to see through
Her iris and pupil smile at me
She winks at one of tenth a second
She waves her fingers tossing up
Honey and pollen stick on her hand
Her fore wing and hind wing wave
Rhythmically to her posture
Cloud looks at me jealous
He comes closer stealthily

His agony squeezes into rain
I am drenched fully
My body shakes inside bed
As sweat emerges from every cell
I close my eyes tightly
Nightmare strikes
Bizarre white light forms into an ellipse
That falls on black screen
Still hold my eyes tightly closed
I suffocate due to lack of oxygen
Pushes the bed sheet off my face
Eerie fever is over…
Now I again tuck myself into bed
To fly to the fairy garden
Future land of no worries
To continue my dream
Ever and forever…

****

15. DON'T JUDGE ME…

The groping incidents in the cities have awakened my
thought to scribble this poem…

Don't Judge Me…
Image result for don't judge me
Home-made red wine rolls
Due to gravity into my tongue
Feelers react wildly
Sends a red alert to brain
Fermented grape juice mixes quickly in the blood
Feel dizzy, Smile mildly
As I feel earth rotation
My mind falls gloomy and thrilled
I bury my head on the couch
Close my eyes to feel ecstasy
Feel lighter and fly above
Walk on city road
Men give a strange look
Some scan with their eyes
I just ignore 'em all
Walk into a mall
A man follows me
His hand comes close
I run into a dressing room of cloth shop
I shock and scream
I'm in a full-length
Mermaid blue Christmas-frock
I realize I'm a girl
I walk out proudly now

Lift a pointed-heel shoe from store racks
Now my legs walk criss-cross
Stalker blows a kiss
Narrowly escape from hitting
Don't judge me…
I'm a free bird
Walkthrough strange men
A glance at my overcoat
See a bike key
Press the start button
Buffalo headed bike comes close
I see my attire changed to jean
With 'Don't enter into my space' t-shirt
Prominent words warn strangers
I wear headgear with plugs
An automated voice asks me for destination
I reply
My voice comes out like I'm singing
Single-wheeled bike rides in auto-mode
Don't come close to me
You're not a reeve…
I sing myself
An automated voice says 'Unwanted comments'
I stop singing and smile
A stranger lifts his left thumb on the road
I stop the bike and he gets on the pillion
I name him 'Dumbo'

As he gives strange looks

Bike picks up pace

Dumbo rolls his hands around my waist

I love the warm feel

My head spins again to remind

I'm single.

Don't want to share my space

I tell him, 'Let's break-up'

Dumbo gives weird look

Don't judge me

You're not a bailie…

It's my world

Why shall I give my space to men?

A warm hand touches my shoulder

Turns back

It's my mom

Stony voice warns me to wake up

I see empty glass with traces of wine

It's my room

I won't allow anyone in…

****

16. EMPTY BENCH...

Enter Caption

My mind oscillates

As I focus on her brown eyes

A string of nerve at forehead aches

I make my hands as a cup

And bury my face into fingers

I turn back to see her

A piece of chalk whisks away

Misses my nose by half a millimetre

My illusion disappears swiftly

The bench is empty

A fraction of a second

Her face and portrait appear

Hears coarse voice behind my ears

Feels like drizzle on my back

As saliva showers in middle of tutor's speech

His angry face looks ghastly

Tutor drags me out of classroom

I shove his hand away

See my bench-mate walks out with me

I stare at him rolling my head

As her voice flows through air

See her image on bench

Gaze on her

Her bosom moves up

As she breathes in

I walk in and sit on her empty seat

Feels like sitting on her lap

Stretches head and neck little back

And lays on her

Closes my eyes, holds breathe

She walks in, stands next to me

I pinch my forearm, 'It's real'

Before I move

She sits on her bench

Narrowly move to my left

To give her space

I bow the head

And turn my gaze at her

Run through her fingers

That shivers unusually

She stands up

Her hanky slips down on ground

I try to lift it to be a 'Good Samaritan'

I see the whole class standing up

Tutor continues to speak

Everyone hides my view

Sudden gloomy shrouds the room

I slide down to take hanky

Her face reads the ground

Eyelids close tightly

I shock to see

As tears roll down her cheeks

Falls down the ground

She breaks down on the desk

Everyone rushes to her

Looks up

Sees a banner on black board

My smiling portrait

Date of birth and death next to me…

****

17. DATING WITH A STRANGER

Enter Caption

It's half past noon

Sun showers in extreme anger

Upon those visible to him

Its end of August

It's like Sun revisits Tropic of Cancer

I ride my 1996-model bike

My mobile rings

I lift the helmet visor

Disconnects the call

My mind voice says

"Will be there in 5 minutes"

Hoping the message flows through the air

To reach her ears

I swim through the traffic

Stops close to an auto-rickshaw

Breeze flows gently

Fresh air fills all air pockets in my body

Feels the blood trail

Pair of hair strands float from the auto-rickshaw

As it nears me

Feels Diana's 'Quelques Fleurs'

Tows bike little forward

To see her

I gaze a gentle look

As the signal turns green, vehicles roll

Narrowly miss the 'miss'

Many overtake my bike

Thanks to the traffic cop
Signal turns red
I park the bike parallel to her
Hastily turn into auto-rickshaw
She rolls her iris, eyelids shutters fast
Her eyes quest for something
I ostensibly turn away my face
Turns back in two seconds
She spills a wry smile
Her fingers flow through the hair
To streamline edgy
I forget to smile back
Turns and smiles at her
She flips her watch twice
I tell: "Don't worry, can board your train"
I guessed right
She twitches her lips
Says: "I was late, only 5 minutes to go"
Read through her lines
She studies in a city college
I ask myself, "Can I offer her a lift?"
I scan through her eyes
She purses her lips
Before I ask, she finishes
"Will you drop me?"
Words choke at the end of my vocal cord
Nods fast, agreeing on her – chewing the words

Dreams a bunch of dancers in uniform dances around me

Before I ask, she says

"Will sit around, if you don't mind"

The signal turns green again

Bike gets momentum

First meeting and

"First dating with a stranger"

I pacify my mind

"She is not a stranger"

The chat continues till a bulky woman come across

She bullies me through her eyes

The girl gets down

Pats at my back,

Spills a 'Thanks'

Runs across to the platform with her yellow back-bag

"Hey", I cried – my words fade out

As volumes of cross-talks fill in the air

Computer-aided woman voice flows through

Announcing a train departure

I turn the bike head

My mind oscillates, "What's her name?"

I stop the bike as 10K-wala crackers

That fills air with thick bluish smoke – choking onlookers

Huge 'thud' noise shakes everyone

Reach office

I see colleagues glue their eyes

On TV "Breaking News"

A panicked journo explains

"Senior space scientist killed in bomb blast"

"Killer woman also dies"

Cameraman pans the visuals of the mangled compartment

I see the torn yellow back-bag

I sink into my chair

Lean back closing my eyes

Feels the hair strands roll on my face

My soul floats in vacuum

Television voice echoes on the background

Is it real or dream…?

****

18. HAPPY NEW YEAR

Enter Caption

I'm at 4,920 ft above sea level

Maancholai;

Creepy insects scream

I come home to celebrate NY-18

No one was there to welcome me

Birds chirp and perch on telescopic treetops

Hear strange noises

Panicked birds make circles in the air

Pivoting to an unknown centre

She emerges from tea leaves

I see her

I jealous of her

Her face glitters in the evening sun

Still young and cheerful

For me.

Many gray hair strands sprout replacing healthy black hairs

I order tea to a vendor

Even he turns old and covers his ears with wool

I meet my mentor after 4 decades

Bhagya Nathan; Tamil teacher

He says she is like TIME

She is the only life never turns old

I understand the truth in life

I can't change her: - TIME

I am getting old everyday

In accordance with the resonance of her

I take a deep breathe

She sneaks into my soul

Switches on my INTEL inside

I feel like elated

My physical appearance may be old

I feel my soul turns younger

I convey my mentor

HAPPY NEW YEAR

****

19. HAPPY PONGAL...

Enter Caption

I walk through the paddy field
It's like watercolour
Green merges with blue – forms sky
Empty white patches turn clouds
People gather at the village temple
Crackers burst the mark of
Pongal fiesta
At Thanneerpallam near Karur
I was with my lensman
To interview an organic farmer…
Someone touches my shoulder
Lift my head
Khaki-clad man speaks like whistling
My soul drops into the real world
I am inside a bus
I see the earth moving backwards
Huge buildings push the bus forward
I am back in the same village
Almost two decades have gone now
I walk down
I see buildings on both sides
No farm and green around me
I stop for a moment
As the temple bell waves and rings
Organic farmer's house with cow farm
Replaced by a commercial complex

Grows taller than two palm trees

I stop near a thatched hut

An old woman walks out

I inquire her, "Do you know organic farmer, who lives here?"

She breaks down into tears

Walk inside the hut

Farmer in 2-D behind festoon

Dirty clothes on string decorate walls

Clothes cover exposing bricks

Traditional Diya's lamp wipes away dark

I keep Pongal present next to lamp

Tears roll down my cheeks

One drop falls on burning Deepam

Fire holds its breath for a wink

And Glows again

Like an efface

I step out

Stumble on a plaque

Nammalvar Street

Black clouds hover around

And it drizzles

Seed droppings on earth

Smile as roots anchor into earth…

****